The Publishers gratefully acknowledge assistance provided by Montego Pomodoro, PhD (pending), chief executive layabout of the National Union of Immature Students, in compiling this book.

Publishers: Ladybird Books Ltd., Loughborough
Printed in England. If wet, Italy.

'How it works'

THE
STUDENT

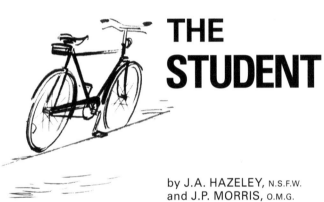

by J.A. HAZELEY, N.S.F.W.
and J.P. MORRIS, O.M.G.

(Authors of 'Owl Do You Do?')

A LADYBIRD BOOK FOR GROWN–UPS

This is a student.

He is leaving home for the first time.

By the time he graduates, he will be a grown-up: exhausted, hideously in debt and unable to imagine going to bed sober.

Reynard has brought everything he needs for his first year.

He unpacks his fancy-dress costumes, his four-way extension leads, his pair of pants and all his didgeridoos.

By doing front, back, inside-out front, inside-out back, and using Febreze and Imodium, he plans to make his pants last until half term.

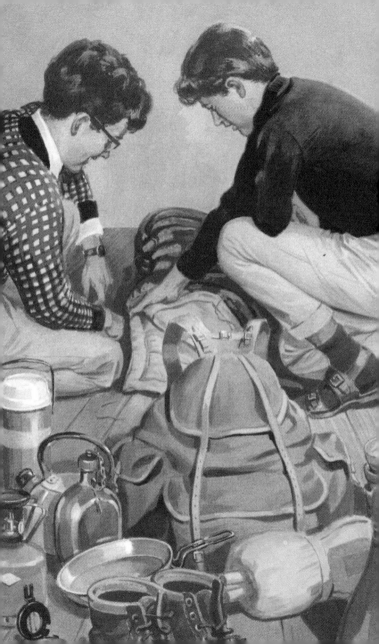

This student accommodation in Derby was built in partnership with Academitas, a subsidiary of the Spanish National Electricity Board.

It has en–suite bathrooms, a gym and well–being centre, and a Magnox fission reactor.

The rooms are certainly nice and warm.

The student's bookshelf has many impressive—looking books.

The books have broken spines and bookmarks in the last page made from tickets to exhibitions and operas, and are full of Post—It notes and pencil marks.

A book can also be made to look well read by washing it.

Lisa finds her revision time-table very tiring.

That is because it starts at 1am, when she can be sure daytime television has definitely finished.

Liam, Wendell and Mork have bought a week's shopping.

To save money for beer, they have not bought toilet paper, bleach, herbs or anything that cannot be eaten or drunk straight from the packaging.

Mork is using his phone to check the recipe for egg.

After four years of work by the students, a new set of no-platforming guidelines has been agreed, and the union building has finally been designated a "safe space".

The wiring was last checked in 1988.

University accommodation can be small, so the student does not need to bring a lot of things from home.

Nina has measured her room, and designed some hand-made furniture that fits just right.

Orson's dissertation is due in tomorrow. He has gone to buy some milk first.

"I could have gone to the shop on campus," thinks Orson, "but then I would not have had all this thinking time."

The Harrods milk is nice, but the last coach back to Sheffield left ten minutes ago.

Nancy had lots of fun during Freshers' Week. She joined the Anti-Nazi League and the Secret Gardeners.

The morning after the Freshers' Ball, she wakes up in a field in northern France.

Nancy apparently also joined Gin Club last night.

Nathan loves pop music. He is studying to be a pop singer at a top performing arts college, with hundreds of other hopeful pop stars.

The course is very expensive, but Nathan imagines a big record deal when he graduates will help him pay off any debts.

Unfortunately, the music industry collapsed in 2006.

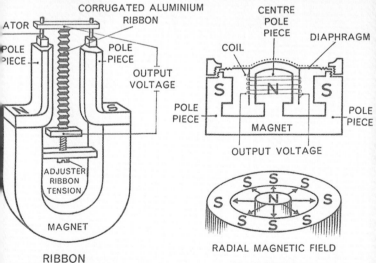

CORRUGATED ALUMINIUM RIBBON

ATOR

POLE PIECE

POLE PIECE

OUTPUT VOLTAGE

ADJUSTER RIBBON TENSION

MAGNET

RIBBON MICROPHONE
(cover removed)

CENTRE POLE PIECE

COIL

DIAPHRAGM

POLE PIECE

S N S

POLE PIECE

MAGNET

OUTPUT VOLTAGE

S S S
S N S
S S S

RADIAL MAGNETIC FIELD

MOVING COIL MICROPHONE

Every time she makes a sandwich, Karen has to make sure her loaf of bread has not gone hard or green.

Karen finds it all quite stressful. After two terms she will give up and switch to cream crackers.

When Karen qualifies as a nurse, she will not mention the difficulty she had looking after bread.

Most of the books she needs for her thesis on the Carolingian Renaissance are out on loan, but Aisha has found a coffee table book of black—and—white photographs of David Beckham, which she has been studying for two and a half hours.

"There is nothing wrong with employing secondary sources," thinks Aisha.

Joanne is a fine art student. She is submitting her coursework in punch—card form to the FINBAR plagiarism computer.

FINBAR contains punch—cards of all art that has ever been made. This card is The Haywain.

If Joanne has just done The Haywain again, the computer will know and she will fail.

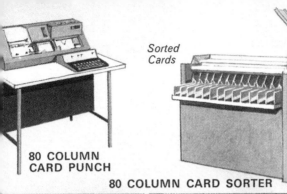

80 COLUMN CARD PUNCH

Sorted Cards

Unsorted Cards

80 COLUMN CARD SORTER

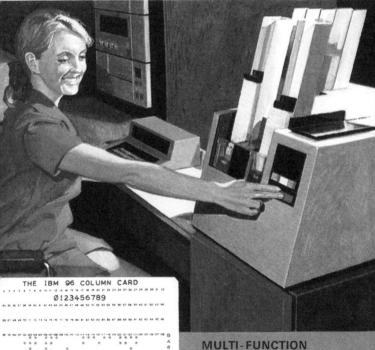

THE IBM 96 COLUMN CARD

Ø123456789

MULTI-FUNCTION CARD UNIT
Punches and sorts 96 Column cards

A 96 COLUMN CARD
(Slightly reduced)

Bramley has found a job that fits round his time—table and earns him extra money for the things he likes.

For every pint of blood Bramley gives, he receives two biscuits, which he can sell.

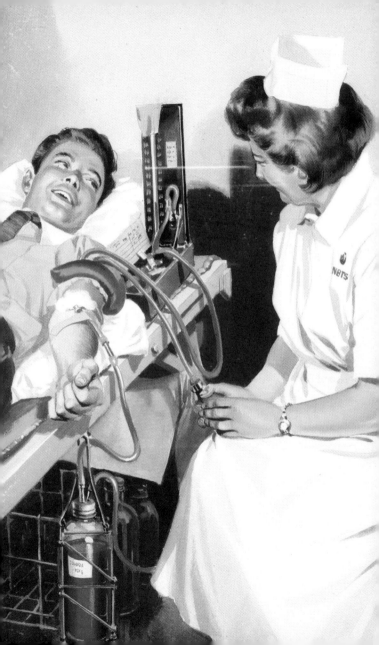

These industrial sausages are cheaper than shop sausages and are big enough to last a whole term.

They are available from the docks or the internet and their fishy afterburn is easily masked with ketchup.

Tito's dissertation is due. He has set himself a target this week of 10,000 words.

So far, he has written 3,500 words, but mainly in the form of passive–aggressive notes to his housemates reminding them who drinks goat's milk and why.

Tandy has paid for a share of a legal high which her flatmate Noz found on Somalian eBay.

The packet has a picture of a sleeping hippopotamus and a red skull with Xs for eyes.

Tandy is sure that if the high were really dangerous Noz would not be stirring quite so much of it into his Doll Noodles.

Lorraine has a long-distance relationship with her boyfriend from back home. He went to another college four hundred miles away.

"I miss you," says Lorraine.

Later Lorraine will cry wine tears into the lap of her housemate Adam. Lorraine thinks Adam is a bit like her boyfriend, but warmer and closer and not on a screen.

Students like to protest. In Paris in 1968, students rioted over the Vietnam War.

Students still protest today. In 2013, four lecturers at Goldsmiths College were hospitalised after a riot about intermittent Wi-Fi coverage.

This fortified Latvian tomato vin—de—guerre has the highest alcohol per penny of anything in the all—night shop.

Megan is going to mix it with blue fizzy pop. In the morning she will only have to clean up her blue vomit, not anyone else's.

It is good to divide up household chores fairly.

Orinoco is telling his new college friends about his gap year in Srinidab.

"Thanks to the bridge I built," he explains, "the orphans could get to the well. Which I also built."

Orinoco actually spent his gap year working in the Basingstoke branch of JJB Sports. There is no such country as Srinidab.

These students are graduating. Each one of them owes over £50,000.

Their degrees will help them get good jobs.

Luckily there are plenty of jobs in the financial industries, servicing record levels of personal debt.

At the graduation ceremony, the student wears a gown and mortar board.

People take lots of photographs of the student in the smart outfit.

This is a good way to remember what the student did not look like at college and never will again.